My Long Journey in Baltimore

by Lawerence E. Mize

DORRANCE
PUBLISHING CO
EST. 1920
PITTSBURGH, PENNSYLVANIA 15238

Dorrance Publishing Co
585 Alpha Drive
Suite 103
Pittsburgh, PA 15238
Visit our website at *www.dorrancebookstore.com*

ISBN: 978-1-6453-0634-4
eISBN: 978-1-6453-0650-4

This book is dedicated to my family, friends, and the many people who have come into and out of my life over the years. They helped shape and make me the man I am today, and I am eternally grateful.

INTRODUCTION

I chose to start this book of poems by going back to when all I knew was the chaos that swirled around me and my family. I can close my eyes and drift back to when I was a chubby little boy running around in West Baltimore. So many images of that time pop into my mind.

I could never put a finger on the exact time when things went wrong for my family. I do, however, remember a short period of time when things were okay. My mom would bake cakes on the weekend and life seemed normal. The elementary school my sister, brothers, and I attended was just across the street from our house. There was work for my dad and we would sometimes go to a park not far away to play.

Things took a turn for the worst when I was around nine or ten. My dad would come home from work later and later in the afternoons smelling of alcohol, and he and my mom would argue. I wrote the poem "See My Daddy Home" on one of those occasions when I would reflect back on when things went wrong for us.

I remember the drinking started when we lived in the 1800 block of Hollins Street. Before long, seeing a pint bottle of Club 400 whiskey on the kitchen table became a regular thing. We began to move from house to house and from one rundown apartment to another. On several occasions I would have to split my skates in half and nail them to the corners of doors we used to move our belongings. By the time I entered junior high school my teachers were calling me the "nomad" because my address changed so much. My dad would sometimes come home drunk with his pockets turned inside out from being "rolled" (robbed) by someone in one of the many bars he frequented. He and my mother would fight and before I knew it the police would show up and arrest my dad for assault on my mom or disorderly conduct. We wound up mostly in the Southwest area of the city.

It was a time of great fear and anxiety for our family. It was the sixties. I started working in a little grocery store below one of the many apartments we lived in back then. On weekends I would take a little shoeshine box I had and walk up and down Baltimore Street, entering the bars along the way to shine shoes for twenty-five cents to get extra spending money. By the time I was sixteen I would come and go as I pleased and bought a little 80cc motorcycle that got me everywhere I needed to go. I also dropped out of high school at sixteen. I used to see older men sitting at barstools in some of the taverns I frequented when shining shoes. I would see them and wonder which direction my life was going, and I decided I didn't want to wind up like those men or my father. I joined the U.S. Army at seventeen and spent a one year tour of duty as a combat medic in the Republic of Vietnam with the 101st Airborne Division.

After completing my military obligation, I returned home and joined the Baltimore City Police Department when I turned twenty-one. I met and married my wife, Sandy, and we started our family.

I began to write little notes and poems to my wife when I worked the midnight shift in the district I worked in in Baltimore City. These notes and poems were thrown into a photo album with the thought that one day I would put them together for a book of poems, which I would dedicate to my wife.

I began to have problems with PTSD in 1983 and sought help at our VA Center here in Baltimore. In 1997, I self-published *Tortured Soul* with American Literary Press and then *Dead Men Calling* in 2002. Both of these works were poems based on my experiences in Vietnam and helped me cope with the issues I was having with PTSD.

In 2009, I was diagnosed with coronary artery disease. I realized that I had not as yet put the notes and poems to my wife in a book of poems. With the help of Tate Publishing & Enterprises I was able to accomplish putting together a book of poems titled *Thoughts of You* in 2011, which I dedicated to my wife, Sandy.

I watched my wife's father suffer with dementia for several years and wrote a poem titled "Dementia," which provided me with the inspiration for *Reflections,* a book of poems on life and dying (Create Space Independent Publishing Platform, 2013).

This book of poems is about my experiences in life and how they took me from the streets of Baltimore to the war in Vietnam and back again.

Several poems speak to the riot and looting in Baltimore in April of 2015 and the aftermath with all its violence in the city since. The city appears to be caught in a deadly cycle of violence with crimes and homicides soaring. Baltimore is a wasteland in some areas with no end to the violence in sight. The last four years have ended with over 300 homicides.

I retired from the Baltimore City Police Department in 1999 and several years later became a District Court Bailiff with the District Court of Maryland as a contract worker. In December of 2018, I decided to finally stop working and enjoy my retirement.

My long journey continues.

CONTENTS

Images 1

See My Daddy Home 2

Club 400 3

Teachers 5

Storm 6

Screaming Eagle 7

Cu Chi 9

Huey 12

Incoming 14

Monsoon 16

Mamma San 17

Smiley Face 18

Recon 21

Dead Men Calling 24

Scream 26

Memories of Nam 28

Collision Course 29

Aftermath 32

2 A.M. Blues 35

Opening 39

Solitude 41

My Baby and 1 42

Children 43

Moobie, Moobie 45

A Perfect Day 46

Beautiful Day 48

My List 49

Winter 51

Bailiff 53

Defendants 55

Violation 56

Hardcore 57

Justice 58

Trip Home 60

B-More 62

The Mayor 63

If Only 64

Baltimore's Schools 66

Monsters 67

Boys' Toys 68

Baltimore Beat 70

Exodus 71

Charm City 72

Down Pimlico Way 74

Ode to Baltimore 76

My Gun 80

Glossary 81

IMAGES

Out of the dark
In the dead of night.
Images appear
Drawn to the light.

Little reminders
Of times long past.
Bringing back memories
That forever last.

Depending on the depth
Of the joy or pain.
The images make you happy
Drive you insane.

They need to be acknowledged
When they come and go.
To be put to rest
Until next they show.

See My Daddy Home

I used to see my Daddy
Walking, tired as tired can be.
I'd look out through a windowpane.
The sight always thrilled me.

He'd have his shoulders in a slouch.
His coat was old and worn.
He carried his tools in a carpenter's box.
They took on so many forms.

I'd wonder at the things he made.
How they'd come to be.
He used to tell me stories of jobs he did.
To try and make me see.

I'd get up to go and greet him.
Then run to see my Daddy home.
He'd grab me with his free arm.
Ask me how my day had gone.

I remembered those few seconds,
As I sat at home today.
A little boy and his dad.
Together at the end of the day.

CLUB 400

I know how it feels,
To be alone.
To suffer in silence
In a chaotic home.

My parents would drink
Whiskey and rum.
Let the alcohol pour
Over their gums.

I never had
The things I'd need.
Went without,
But, they could never see.

They never saw
The hurt in my eyes.
They never heard
The times I'd cry.

I used to think
It was all my fault.
A kid in the way
Right from the start.

I'd wake each day,
To see a bottle of booze.
Old Club 400
The same tired news.

The day would end
The way it began.
If I knew where to go
I would have ran.

Time's moved on.
They're both in their graves.
I carried on,
Somehow saved.

Got a good life.
Family and friends.
Some haven't a clue.
As to where I've been.

I see others
With the same kind of pain.
Lost in the sickness,
With nothing to gain.

I want them to know.
They can persevere.
Keep looking to tomorrow.
A new day without fear.

Teachers

Some of the best people
I've ever known
Were teachers who cared.
Made me feel at home.

They chose not to look
At my ragged threads,
Or ask about the chaos
Swirling about in my head.

They gave me a sliver of lead
In a piece of wood.
To mark the way
So I understood.

The years came and went
As I grew and learned.
They were always there
With me at every turn.

I often think
Of where I might be,
If not for the teachers
Who cared about me.

STORM

Gray billowing clouds
Rolled over the land.
A gentle breeze
Brought by God's hand.

The wind kissed the leaves
As branches swayed.
The sky grew dark
As the light began to fade.

I breathed in the air.
Smelled the rain.
Watched the lighting.
It's always the same.

Sat for a while
Until I heard the thunder.
Gazed up at the sky,
It was such a wonder.

Thought of the things
I've lived to see.
Comforting to know
God's walked with me.

SCREAMING EAGLE

I'm a Screaming Eagle.
A real puking buzzard.
I come from the air
To destroy and smother.

Use rotors for wings.
Come in smoking.
Land in the boonies,
Tell ya man, I'm not joking.

Set up a perimeter.
Secure the LZ.
Start an assault.
Look for VC.

I go up and down valleys.
Recon in the bush.
Plow through the jungle.
Don't need no push.

Walk in the vills.
Down beaten paths.
Worm through the tunnels.
I'm here to kick ass.

I'm young and I'm strong.
As hardcore as they come.
Humping in the Nam.
Keep Charlie on the run.

Cu Chi

Cu Chi

Cu Chi was a bitch,
Believe me, I know.
Broke my cherry.
Made me grow.

Transformed me from a street punk
From good old Baltimore.
God aided the change,
A child no more.

Rounds started dropping.
Seemed so near.
Thought I'd be okay.
Thought our guys knew we were here.

I saw a cloud of dirt fill the air.
Heard men screaming loud and clear.
Grabbed my aid-kit, taking off in a run.
Went through the cloud that blocked the sun.

Once in the commotion
saw a lot of guys down.
Corpses and wounded,
Spread out all over the ground.

I kneeled by the wounded
And started my IVs.
Used up my bandages.
Wondered how many there could be.

My morphine syrettes
Were gone in a flash.
I only had five.
Knew they wouldn't last.

The shock of what happened
Was met with disbelief.
Realized I was at war
with so much time to do.

Huey

HUEY

Tiny speck
In the sky.
Drawing nearer.
Flying high.

Thump, thump, thump,
rotor blades beating.
Bringing hope.
Set fears fleeting.

Joined by others
Forming a V.
Headed for the LZ.
Headed for me.

Smoke popping.
Its odor fouls the air.
I feel invincible.
No longer care.

My lifelines back
Growing ever so larger.
Green and ugly.
I love it dearly.

The Huey dives for the ground.
Then flares out above the grass.
I take my leave.
Quickly deass.

I climb aboard.
Take my place.
Forget the terrible things
I've had to face.
I'm inbound for home.

Hue, Bien Hoa, Cu Chi.
Their names don't matter.
The Huey has me.

I rise above the trees.
Watch the ground rush past.
Airborne again.
Flying so fast.

INCOMING

They opened up
As we crossed the field.
We were caught in the open
With no tree line in which to steal.

Their rounds struck the mud.
Mortars fell in behind.
We scattered like roaches.
Fell in the rice paddy slime.

Shouts of "Incoming!"
Filled the air.
With nowhere to run
It didn't seem fair.

I listened for sounds
Of "Medic" or "Doc."
Didn't want to die here.
Didn't want to rot.

The radio crackled
From the RTO's back.
They had got us good.
Trapped us like rats.

With nowhere to run.
No vill in which to hide.
I raced to the wounded.
Bagged those that died.

Forgot my fears
As I kept on the move.
Was afraid to stop.
Knew my life I would lose.

The attack continued on
For a half-hour or so.
Then as if by magic,
Stopped...don't you know.

The rice paddy grew quiet
save for the moans.
No more shouts of "Incoming!"
Only pissed-off groans.

MONSOON

Can't stand the rain.
Drives me insane.
Dulls the senses.
Fucks with the brain.

Balls are itching.
Skin's on fire.
Feet swollen and wet.
Hate walking through the muck and mire.

It's hard to see
Through the torrential downpour.
Soaks everything in sight.
Then rains some more.

They call it the "Monsoon"
Comes every year.
Something the Vietnamese
Hold very dear.

It fills the paddies
Where rice grows in the flooded fields.
Sustains the country
for yet another year.

It continues to fall
As we fight in the vills.
The ground soaks it up.
Can't get its fill.

It comes to cleanse
And wash away
A soldier's blood
At the end of the day.

Mamma San

Mamma San smiles
With blackened teeth.
Washes my clothes.
Gives me things to eat.

We barter and trade
For the strangest things.
She's looking for a deal.
It's always the same.

She'll sell her body,
but not her soul.
Possesses an ageless beauty.
Keeps her heart cold.

I see her in vills
With a toothless grin.
Squatting by hootches
Sorry to see me again.

She fills sandbags by day.
Carries an AK at night.
She'll fight for her cause.
She knows she's right.

I see her in basecamps.
Down dusty roads.
Out in the paddies.
She carries a heavy load.

She's the strength of her country.
Can't break her will.
I'm just another intruder
Walking through her fields.

SMILEY FACE

I went to Bien Hoa
To see a wounded friend.
Walked to the Aid-Station
Inquired within.

Was met by a nurse.
Her smile so big and warm.
She led me to his bed.
Told me how he's been.

I stayed for a while
Conversing with my friend.
Heard a Huey land outside.
Saw the wounded being rushed in.

I looked about for a while.
The nurse seemed quite busy.
She tended the wounded.
The place was in a frenzy.

The commotion continued
For an hour or so.
I told my friend
It was time for me to go.

I walked by a room
so quiet and still.
The nurse stood alone.
Looked a little ill.

A soldier lay dead
On a bloodied army cot.
Nothing could have saved him
From his horrific shot.

The smile was gone from her beautiful face.
A frown was there instead, in its place.
She wiped at a tear
That suddenly rolled down.

I continued on
Being ever so quiet.
Fearful another copter
would start a riot.

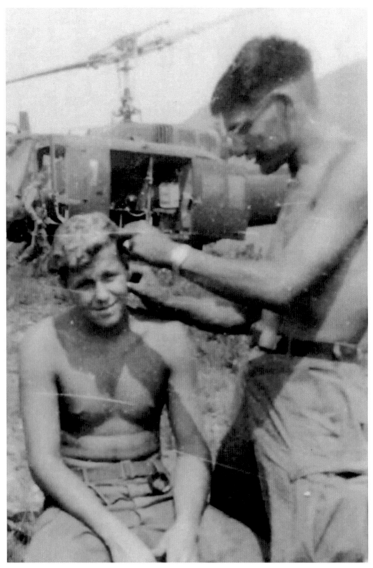

Author getting a haircut from Senior Aidman Keith Marshall
on Geronimo

RECON

I covered every position.
Gave each man his big orange pill.
I was greeted with friendly smiles
As I made my way around the hill.

Everyone was happy.
We were again in the rear.
A few called out to tease me:
"Hey, Doc! Why did you give me this pill?"

I checked their sores and blisters
brought on by heavy rucksacks.
No one seemed to mind.
There was nothing they lacked.

Geronimo, we called it.
Home was this lonely hill.
Malaria was a threat,
Hence the pill.

Everything was to be forgotten
While we drank and ate our fill.
Burning shit and standing guard,
There was nothing to fear.

Geronimo was safety.
A place to let go.
A much needed break from humping.
God, if you could only know.

We had lain around and took it easy.
Letting the sun dry our clothes.
With darkness came the Lieutenant,
His arrival meant it was nearly time to go.

I readied my aid-kit.
Then drew tight the straps.
I made a mental note of everything in it,
While I prayed my supplies would last.

We moved out in single file.
Staring at the back of the last man's head.
I couldn't help but wonder,
Who would be among the dead.

The night seemed to drag on forever,
Until we set up in a circle near a well-traveled path.
We put out our tripflares and claymores
Setting our deadly trap.

We lay on the ground and waited.
Looking out into the night.
Hoping it would prove uneventful.
That we could rejoice in the oncoming light.

We heard them coming.
Singing as they walked down the path.
Unconsciously I tensed every muscle
Anticipating the imminent bloodbath.

They tripped the flares
Appearing as dark shadows in the artificial light.
They ran about confused,
Searching for the night.

They reached for their rifles
Slung on their backs.
I hit my claymore and saw the blast.
I knew the man in front of me had breathed his last.

We pulled back to hide
In this deadly game of cat-and-mouse.
When morning came we went back for the count.
Three dead NVA lay in the grass.

They seemed so young.
Ageless, if you will.
I felt numb all over.
Unable to feel.

We humped back to Geronimo.
Our home in the rear.
We were all glad to be alive.
The recon was no big deal.

Nowhere could the word be heard...KILL.

DEAD MEN CALLING

I see their faces.
Hear their shouts.
Long-dead soldiers
Calling me out.

They stand in a group
Atop a hill.
Smile as if posing.
So lifeless and still.

Uniforms so dirty.
Streaked with red.
Such wicked smiles
From the long-past dead.

I know these men.
They were once there for me.
Keep returning in my sleep.
Won't let me be.

They died so young.
In horrible fashion.
For some…
In their very first action.

I've tried to distance myself
From that period in time.
Let Vietnam go.
It was never really mine.

It continues to cling.
Grab and hold.
The memories come in a flood
As I continue to grow old.

So there they stand
Atop that damn hill.
Waiting for "Old Doc"
Their final kill.

SCREAM

At night I scream...
A lonely high-pitched wail.
That curdles the blood
Straight out of hell.

I see men die.
Mourn the loss.
Jesus left me.
He's faceless on my cross.

I look around.
Watch the fog roll in.
Feel the rain
So cold on my skin.

A Huey appears.
Tiny speck in the sky.
I sit alone.
Wondering why.

The taste of death
So fresh on my lips.
No one to save me
From this nightmarish trip.

VC in the grass
And on the hills.
VC in the treetops
Waiting to kill.

I hear the thump, thump of rotors
Beating the air.
Pop my smoke
Without a care.

I roll them and pack them
Into green body bags.
Lifeless and heavy
They always sag.

I wait for the bird
To come rushing down.
To take my load.
Get them off the ground.

Their numbers don't matter.
Dead is dead.
It's always their faces
Stuck in my head.

I lay asleep.
Caught in this wretched dream.
No one to hear me
As I scream and scream.

Nam was a place
So real and strange.
Stripped you naked.
Filled you with shame.

Memories of Nam

I watched them fall
And then they died.
Bagged them up.
Fought hard not to cry.

Supply ships rolled in
Carried them away.
I packed my aid-kit.
Prepared for another day.

Some only lasted
For just a little while.
Their dead eyes blank;
No clue they ever smiled.

They'd come in a rush.
Died in a flash.
I was one of the few
Who made it to the last.

I counted the days
Till it was time to go.
They took forever,
Passed so slow.

The memories of Nam
continue to come.
Leaving me no place to go.
Nowhere to run.

COLLISION COURSE

On a collision course.
Don't know why.
Thoughts of Nam
Make me cry.

Cast adrift
In a sea of the past.
PTSD has claimed me.
Lord, long at last.

Don't know where I'm going.
Only where I've been.
Memories of Nam
Keep reeling me in.

Older now,
Haven't grown.
Stuck in Southeast Asia
Hearing helpless moans.

Saw men die.
Bore witness to it all.
Like sticks of wood
They had to fall.

Feel the shame
For what I've done.
No one to blame;
I'm the only one.

Bear the guilt for leaving
Those I had come to know.
I had to live.
They had to go.

I didn't pick
And couldn't choose.
God took his numbers.
They flashed them on the news.

Want to let go.
Be rid of the dreams.
Forget the faces.
Turn off the screams.

I struggle to cope
Try to blend in.
Be like everyone else.
Forget where I've been.

I'm a cook, a cop...
Neighbor's best friend.
Searching for answers.
Waiting for the end.

Some call me hero.
Don't know why.
I fought to live.
Tried hard not to die.

I've survived.
Made it this far.
Fight the urge
To belly up to a bar.

I stand on corners.
Holding my sign.
Beg for pennies.
Committing no crimes.

I'm housed in prisons
All across the land.
Say, brother…
Won't you lend me a hand?

I'm at the VFW.
American Legion, too.
Joined the many.
Part of the few.

I want to understand.
Know the why.
My friends…my friends
Had to die.

AFTERMATH

The war is long over.
The one we never won.
No cheers of joy.
Just broken men on the run.

Branded as outcasts.
Stereotyped as ticking bombs.
Only wanted to serve our country.
Return home to our moms.

So analyzed and debated
To find at whose feet lay the blame.
Yet there's no one to latch on to
To account for all the names.

Names etched in stone.
On a shiny granite wall.
If only they could speak
They'd tell it all.

They'd speak of their pain and suffering.
The lost chance for fame.
There would be no excuses.
Nothing to sound lame.

Now it's just us old-timers.
The ones who have had their fill.
Stuck with horrible memories.
Served up a bitter pill.

We did our duty.
Served our country well.
Left only with stories
Too terrible to tell.

We searched for the enemy.
Never had to go far.
Caused so much damage.
Left so many scars.

We fought to win
While others at home played games.
They made their decisions.
Some hid behind their names.

The cowards at home
Wore their silly peace signs.
Burned their draft cards.
Sang their little rhymes.

Songs of protest
Filled the air.
Joints of pot
Appeared everywhere.

Marches and chants.
Nasty rumors of war.
Dirty little subversives
Hiding in every door.

Some of the rats fled to Canada.
Others were deferred.
Now they seek glory.
Run for office...want to serve.

A shot in the head
Should be a traitor's just reward.
The cowards should have been branded
like cattle in a herd.

They gave us nothing
When they were young.
Now they want power.
Feel safe enough to run.

Their smiles so sincere.
Promises so great.
Just want your vote.
Know they'll skate.

It's over for us.
The men and women of our kind.
We served our country with courage.
In blood we did our time.

2 A.M. Blues

It's 2 A.M., I'm feeling blue.
Roused from bed.
Memories of Nam
Drifting through.

Time again.
To put pen to pad.
Write of things
That make me sad.

Want to let go.
Put it all to rest.
It's enough to know
I passed life's test.

Shake with dread
From the flooding thoughts.
Put names to faces
Of those who were lost.

No glory for me.
Or those who served.
Branded "Baby Killers,"
Of all the nerve.

Relive a time
So long ago.
Envision a place.
I had come to know.

Search and Destroy
Was the name of the game.
Large body counts
Brought recognition and fame.

All the battles we fought
In places quickly forgotten.
The stench of death
So putrid and rotten.

Napalm canisters
Tumbling through the air.
Instant horror.
Dropped with care.

Villes and hootches
Burned to the ground.
Plenty of pain
To go around

Tag'em and bag'em.
Our brothers in arms.
Their numbers at home.
Brought such an alarm.

They died from our guns.
Malaria took a few.
Snipers and mines,
Mortars too.

So senseless it was.
The little war we had.
All the people killed,
It's enough to make you go mad.

It's 2 A.M., I'm feeling blue.
Another sleepless night.
Nothing new.

Sweeping for Mines

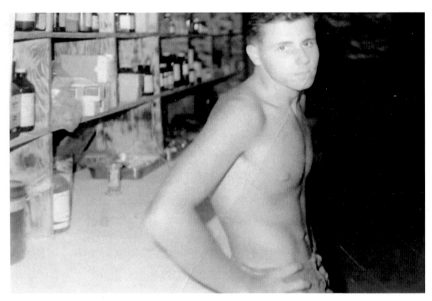

Author in Aid-Station at LZ Sally
Republic of Vietnam, 1968

OPENING

I let a crack
Open the seal.
Hurt poured out
Showed how I feel.

Wanted to keep
Everything bottled in.
But, thought I'd trust
A newfound friend.

The words came out
In a torrential rush.
Only my sobs
Could make me hush.

Once a hurt
Is given a vent,
A weight is lifted
leaving you spent.

The crack grows wide
Letting the heart heal.
Leaving you wondering,
"What was the big deal?"

SOLITUDE

The fading winter
Whispered in my ears.
Billowing clouds
Threatened to spill.

I rode alone
As often is the case.
Felt the cold
Pressing on my face.

The trees stood tall
Bare of their leaves.
Sentinels standing guard
As far as I could see.

No one in sight
For quite a few miles.
The comfort of my solitude
Brought on a warming smile.

I rode on and on.
Far and away.
Thanked the Lord
For giving me this day.

My Baby and I

Watched the wife
Earlier tonight.
Head bobbing
Eyes shut tight.

She looked so tired.
All worn down.
I tried to be quiet,
Didn't make a sound.

My baby and I
Have been such a pair.
We cling to each other
Because we care.

The years have been long,
But we made it through.
My baby and I,
Somehow we knew.

Knew that our love
Would carry the day.
Give us strength
To make our way.

Now we've arrived
At that time in our life.
Happy with "us"
To warm our nights.
My baby and I.

CHILDREN

Little eyes
Pierce your soul.
Gives you meaning
To want to grow old.

Their laughter comes
To welcome the day.
Have so much going on
And lots to say.

They give you their trust.
Let you see their tears.
With Mom and Dad
They know no fear.

Children fill your heart
With joy and love.
Make you want to reach out
To give them a big hug.

MOOBIE, MOOBIE

It started one day
Many years ago.
Me and the kids
Traveling the high road.

We went to the movies
To see the shows.
I pronounced it "Moobie, Moobie."
That's what they came to know.

We'd spend the day
Out of a long weekend.
Me, the kids,
Sometimes a friend.

The trip was an adventure
For them and me.
A happy bunch
For all to see.

Now I'm old
Kids are grown.
Not unhappy.
No need to moan.

My oldest son
Still goes with me.
Now the grandkids
Get treated to a "Moobie."

Lucky man
I truly am.
Traveling the high road
Once again.

A Perfect Day

Days in June
Are like no other.
Sunshine, kids,
Weddings of wonder.

The joining of two hearts
To beat as one.
A life's adventure
Only just begun.

I enjoy these events
On warm summer days.
See hope for the future,
In oh so many ways.

The harbor looked great
On this beautiful day.
Perfect for a wedding
In every way.

I looked around.
Took in the sights.
Boats in the water.
Birds in flight.

Baltimore was alive.
Vibrant and strong.
A city on the move.
In June nothing goes wrong.

Ladies in fine dresses.
Men in classy attire.
The restaurant was jumping.
I sat at the bar.

I took it all in,
As I usually do.
A poet and his pen.
Not something new.

Lauren was stunning.
In her bridal dress.
Gary looked sharp,
A man at his best.

We waited their arrival.
There was hardly a sound.
The ceremony was held
Inside the lounge.

The vows they shared
Would last a life.
Congrats to Gary and Lauren.
Now husband and wife.

BEAUTIFUL DAY

A beautiful day
Out in the sun.
Doing chores,
getting things done.

Counted my blessings
As I gazed at the sky.
No more rain.
I'm a lucky guy.

Grandkids came.
We played catch in the yard.
Living so easy.
Nothing seemed hard.

Perfect it was
And I stopped to rest.
Thanked the Lord
For making it one of his best.
This beautiful day.

My List

If I could ask
For a few things in life.
The top of my list
Would name my wife.

She's seen me through
So many years.
Laughed with me.
Shed some tears.

Of course my sons
Would follow her lead.
I'd have to see
To their every need.

They give me joy
Only a father would know.
Made me proud
As I watched them grow.

Next the women
Who made them whole.
Took them away
Just as I was getting old.

Now my grandchildren
Who call me Pop.
That's my list
From bottom to top.

Lucky was I
To hold so much wealth.
All I needed
Was the love I felt.

You need a list
To help make your way.
Give you focus
To live another day.

WINTER

Back porch furniture
All put away.
Leaves raked, lawn mowed.
Such a wonderful day.

No more long rides
With the wind as my only sound.
The feel of winter
Bearing down.

Long, dark nights
Filled with cold ahead.
Earmuffs, gloves, coats,
Shovels in the shed.

A time to be merry.
Filled with the spirit of Christ.
Watch snowflakes fall
In the waning light.

Winter's joy
Measured in a frozen kiss.
The words I Love You.
Spoken from another's lips.

The cold brings the heat.
To warm the heart.
Ah, winter, at last.
It starts.

BAILIFF

I work in a courthouse.
I'm a bailiff, you see.
People come from all over.
Pass by people just like me.

The courtrooms fill up.
People everywhere I see.
Lots and lots of people.
They try to ignore me.

Some have escorts.
Others come alone.
Still others hang in hallways,
Talking on their cellphones.

They are all kinds of people.
In all kinds of dress.
Worried about their future.
How to clean up their life's mess.

Don't want to sound dispositive.
That sure ain't like me.
I feel for these people.
Some are sad as can be.

I have a job to do
No matter what the case.
Protect the judge and keep the peace.
Regardless of the pace.

The job can be boring,
But interesting as well.
Hear and see people play our their woes.
They all have stories to tell.

I stand by the judge.
Whoever he or she may be.
Whenever they render a harmful verdict,
That's when people notice me.

DEFENDANTS

"All rise!" I yell
At the start of the day.
When going to court,
It's the defendants who pay.

Sometimes I peer
At the shaky knees.
The look of fear
And unease.

Faces blank.
Eyes staring straight ahead.
Trying to remember
Words once said.

The chains and cuffs
That bind and chafe.
Steals their identity.
Makes us safe.

Accused they are.
Come to plead their case.
Make a deal.
Get back in the race.

Some prove innocent.
Walk away free.
Others found guilty,
Still can't see.

The harm that's done.
To you and me…
And doing the time
That's never free.

VIOLATION

Saw a pretty girl
In an office today.
Her eyes were on fire.
Not sure what to say.

Her probation officer sat
Cradling the phone.
Said, "Take her now,
She's not going home."

In violation she was
For disobeying the court.
The cuffs went on.
Her liberty cut short.

So off she went,
Back to jail.
Once again,
She had failed.

Hard to stay clean.
Walk that straight line.
Two steps forward.
One behind.

HARDCORE

He walked in the room.
Shackled and cuffed.
Tattoos everywhere.
He looked like a thug.

Life in the lockup
Had kept his nerves on edge.
Dealing with the chaos
Messed with his head.

The State had a deal.
He'd walk away free.
Take a Stet.
Let things be.

Over in a flash.
He felt so relieved.
No need to be hardcore.
Finally at ease.

A scene in the courthouse
Played out this day.
A man in trouble
Finding his way.

JUSTICE

Looked at the back
Of the third-row pew.
"Bitch" scratched in the wood.
What can you do?

The cases were called
In a monotonous tone.
The lawyers and defendants
Came together and alone.

I stood on the side.
At the front of the court.
Listening to the cases.
The endless reports.

A typical day.
Like so many others.
Filled with deals for the accused.
It was all such a wonder.

"Can we approach?"
Was the constant refrain.
Deals made at the bench
Always a shame.

Didn't look good
For the victims of crime.
The constant sidebars
Wasted so much time.

Of all the cases called
On this long docket day.
No one went to jail
Believe what I say.

They come and they go.
In an endless stream.
This is real life.
Though you'd think it a dream.

Probation and fines
Was the order of the day.
Justice is truly blind.
What more can you say?

TRIP HOME

Felt the chill
Upon my bones,
As I left work
Headed home.

Outside was dark.
The day gone.
Just me and my thoughts.
The ride long.

Thought of what
Some mean to me.
Family, friends,
People I see.

They kept me company
As I made my way.
Helped me finish
Another day.

Time sped by.
Never felt alone.
They kept me warm
Until I made it home.

300 Block South Smallwood St.

B-More

Want to yell.
Want to scream.
All the shootings.
Wasted dreams.

Baltimore's caught
In an endless cycle.
Homicides climbing.
Where is St. Michael?

We need some help
From our heavenly hosts.
No time to back off.
No time to coast.

The city's awash.
With victims' blood.
Have to stop
This senseless flood.

The clock is ticking.
Marking time.
This genocide
Is such a crime.

THE MAYOR

The mayor did nothing.
As they tore Baltimore apart.
From Reisterstown Mall
To downtown's very heart.

The rioters ran amok
All through the streets.
Threw rocks at the cops
Whenever they'd meet.

Set fire to buildings.
Gutted stores.
Danced on police cars.
Destroyed a whole lot more.

I watched at home.
Wondered when it would all end.
Felt bad for the people,
Afraid and locked in.

Arrests should have been made
At the very start.
Could have called up the Guard.
Let the governor do his part.

Now the city's a wasteland.
Filled with trash and debris
The mayor's gone.
Hooray and whoopee.

IF ONLY

Homicides keep coming.
Quick as one, two, three.
Thugs were given the city.
Cops had to take a knee.

The legacy of a mayor
So plain to see.
Violence and hatred
It had to be.

Can't give up control.
Can't let chaos rein.
People will die.
It's not a game.

How many souls
Must fade away
In pools of blood,
Both night and day?

In alleys and streets.
Businesses too.
Numbers keep mounting.
Nothing new.

Need a program.
That's the thing to do.
Do-gooders got the answer.
Tell me something new.

Houses worth millions
All vacant and burned.
The city's a wasteland.
Needs to take a new turn.

If only it would stop.
For just a little while.
Give people a break.
Let them smile.

If only, if only,
Crime took a back seat.
They could clean up the city.
Make it all bright and neat.

If only, if only,
No one else had to die.
No mothers or wives left alone
Would ever have to cry…if only.

BALTIMORE'S SCHOOLS

The schools are failing.
City schools are a mess.
No more cursive writing.
No more being the best.

No heat in the winter.
Not cool when it's hot.
Kids have to worry.
Afraid they might get shot.

The guns keep coming.
School police unarmed.
Tough to protect them.
Keep them from harm.

You fail, they pass you.
Can't leave you behind.
Don't have to learn.
Just graduate when it's time.

So much money spent
Year after year.
Educators dooming students.
Never shedding a tear.

Out into the world
The wretched ones go.
The diplomas they carry
Are only for show.

MONSTERS

Monsters are here.
The ones we never see.
They lay in wait for victims.
Victims like you and me.

They hang out on corners.
At stores near malls.
They'll take your possessions.
Your money and cars.

Time means nothing.
They hit day and night.
The monsters are coming.
Got you in their sights.

Some use guns.
Others brute force.
They get you cornered.
You haven't a choice.

They are somebody's kids.
They can kill you too.
These Baltimore juveniles...
Monsters, coming for you.

Boys' Toys

These lookalike guns
Being used today
Are toys of destruction,
Making Robbery a game of play.

Not so bad
When they get the dough.
The poor, the weak, the dumb,
give it up and go.

But when the victims are armed
And don't want to play,
These stupid robbers get shot,
Become the talk of the day.

Shouts of "Why'd they shoot?"
Fill the air.
When it's a kid lying dead
They scream, "Unfair!"

The news will portray them
As kids on the go.
With futures so bright,
It's a sin, don't you know?

If larceny is in your heart.
And you really don't care,
You might fool most.
But, one might dare.

Dare to challenge.
Dare to fight back.
Whether a kid or an adult,
No one will have your back.

The barrel of a gun
Can make your mind race.
You see your life flash
In front of your face.

Ought to outlaw toys
That look so real.
Tell your kids
They can get them killed.

BALTIMORE BEAT

No more sitting
Out on the stoop.
No more ballplaying.
Throwing hoops.

Cops and judges.
People from the street.
Everywhere you look
They all seem beat.

Homicides are rising
Crime is picking up.
Summer's coming.
The pain is gonna suck.

There are no easy answers
To the problems of our day.
Folks are getting angry
Doing things the same old way.

Thugs keep stealing.
Dealers cashing in.
Psychopaths keep killing.
In Baltimore nobody wins.

EXODUS

The exodus continues.
People continue to flee.
Baltimore's getting empty.
Politicians just can't see.

No one wants to be a victim.
Just want to be left alone.
Afraid to walk about.
Afraid to leave home.

They make it so hard.
On the working poor.
High taxes, traffic cameras,
Parking control agents galore.

The city's got its hands
In everyone's pockets.
The people are leaving
Fast as a rocket.

Crime's still soaring.
People still getting shot.
Won't be much longer
Before Baltimore's one big empty lot.

CHARM CITY

Another commissioner leaving.
Need someone new for the top.
The grinder keeps on grinding,
Chewing up all the cops.

Thugs be a-smiling.
No matter what the city do,
They gonna "get them some."
The change ain't nothing new.

Streets are looking bleak.
Panic rules the day.
Druggies need a hit.
It's the same old play.

Shorty's on the corner.
Got some "stuff' to sell.
The wretched keep a-coming.
No need for him to yell.

It happens in the open.
No more hiding behind closed doors.
They come with money ready.
The crooks, the whores.

They call it Charm City.
Good old Baltimore.
The people who know better
See it as a revolving door.

Some get lucky.
Move up and out.
Others just be stuck,
Want to scream and shout.

There's no "charm" in the city.
No one knows what to do.
Be careful when you visit.
Don't become a victim too.

DOWN PIMLICO WAY

I used to love
To hear my boss say,
"Hey, Larry, want to go
to the track today?"

We'd hop in his car
After closing the store.
Then off to the track;
Who could ask for more?

I remember a race
From so long ago.
I bet on Dear Doc,
Two dollars for show.

I ran to the rail
To watch the horses run.
I was just thirteen.
Pimlico was so much fun.

The race was fast
As they rounded the turn.
Dear Doc had the lead
In the midday sun.

He went on to win.
I was happy as could be.
The track was an adventure
So exciting for me.

Now, I look back and remember
How great Pimlico had been.
Seeing it in its demise
Seems like such a sin.

The city will lose the preakness
To another track.
So sad to know,
In Baltimore…nothing lasts.

ODE TO BALTIMORE

Rode by houses
I lived in, in the day.
Now boarded-up relics,
Wood rot and decay.

Streets were empty.
No people about.
No children playing.
No happy shouts.

Thought of a time
Not so long ago
When Baltimore was alive
With families on the go.

People dreamed dreams.
Were neighborly and nice.
Now they seem mean
With blood cold as ice.

Down Wilhelm to Smallwood Streets.
Places in between.
Trash and debris,
Streets not so clean.

Saddened by the sights
I saw today.
Just didn't seem right.
Should never be okay.

I pulled onto Wilkens Ave.
To drive out of town.
Left Baltimore behind.
A city going down.

2200 Block Wilkens Ave. – Even Side

2000 Block Willhelm Street – Even Side

2000 Block Wilhelm Street – Odd Side

My Gun

The rain came down hard
Striking the pavement and stone.
I looked out into the night.
I was chilled to the bone.

I could feel my gun
Weigh heavy on my hip.
Wondered at the time,
Would it be a fast or slow shift?

I've worn a gun
Most of my life.
A necessary tool
That always felt right.

The gun's always there,
No matter what I do.
A gentle reminder
To help me get through.

The years came and went.
My tools changed with the times.
From six-shot revolvers
To semi-automatic nines.

It goes with the badge
I wear on my chest.
I'm one of the many
Doing their best.

I've always thought
Of how great it would be
If there was never a need
For people like me.

GLOSSARY

Bailiff	Retired police officer or deputy sheriff
Basecamp	Operational area utilized by soldiers
Charlie	Term for enemy soldiers
Huey	Nickname for UH-1 helicopters
LZ	Landing zone for helicopters
Medic	Soldier who provides medical aid to injured soldiers
Mamma San	Term used for Vietnamese women
Monsoon	Rainy season
Morphine syrettes	Painkiller carried by medical corpsmen
NVA	North Vietnamese Army
Napalm	Jelly-like incendiary substance used in bombs
Recon	Reconnaissance missions
Screaming Eagle	Soldier of the 101st Airborne Division
Stet	Once accepted by the defendant, the case is placed on an inactive docket and a person gives up his/her right to a speedy trial. It can be reopened at any time in the first year and can be expunged from a person's record after three years.
VC	Viet Cong

Lawerence E. Mize was born in Baltimore, Maryland, in 1949. At the age of seventeen he enlisted in the U.S. Army. Nearly a month after his eighteenth birthday he began his one-year tour of duty in the Republic of Vietnam. He served with the "Screaming Eagles" of the 101st Airborne Division as a combat medic. On completing his military obligation he returned to Baltimore, where he joined the Baltimore City Police Department. Mize went on to serve nearly thirty years with the Baltimore City Police Department, retiring as a Sergeant in 1999. Mize became a District Court Bailiff in 2003.

Mize has self-published four books of poetry since 1997, to include two works, *Tortured Soul* and *Dead Men Calling,* which helped him deal with the painful memories of Vietnam; a book of poems he dedicated to his wife, Sandy, *Thoughts of You,* after having been diagnosed with coronary artery disease; and *Reflections,* a book of poems on life and dying.

My Long Journey in Baltimore is a culmination of Mize's life in poems.

Mize is married to his wife, Sandra, to whom he has been married since 1973. Lawerence and Sandy have two sons and three grandchildren.